The Midwood Collection

Classic images of Ramsey and the North

All images are Midwood, except where credited.

Stacking up glass plate negatives at the rear of Midwood's studio on South Prom.
Left to right: Dan Joughin, Lily Midwood, May Midwood, Eric Tregellis, Charlie Midwood.
(courtesy Ken Hassell)

Published by:
Lily Publications, PO Box 33,
Ramsey, Isle of Man IM99 4LP
Tel: +44 (0) 1624 898446 Fax: +44 (0) 1624 898449
E-mail: info@lilypublications.co.uk
Website: www.lilypublications.co.uk

Photographic research team:
Les Clarke, Ray Stanfield and Sue Woolley

Foreword

THE Directors and Staff of Harding Lewis Limited are delighted to be associated with the *Midwood Collection*. We have been involved in the life of Ramsey and the surrounding villages for many years, helping businesses and individuals to prosper and grow.

However, the Midwoods have an even closer connection to Harding Lewis, as one of our Directors Debra Cooper is a great-niece of Thomas Horsfall (T.H.) Midwood, who was a half brother of her great-grandmother, Helena Midwood. Helena and Thomas were the children of Charles James Midwood, who was born in Manchester and married four times, with three of his wives buried in the Isle of Man. Thomas inherited his father's photographic equipment.

We hope you enjoy the *Collection*.

Harding Lewis, Shannon Court,
Bowring Road, Ramsey,
Isle of Man IM8 2LQ
Tel: 01624 812343
Fax: 01624 816914
www.hardinglewis.com

Another 'big catch' landed at the fish steps.

Introduction

FOR three quarters of a century, the social history of Ramsey and the northern parishes was captured by Midwood photographers.

Here we present a selection of images chronicling life in Ramsey and the northern parishes from the late Victorian era to the end of the Second World War. For this we are indebted to Les Clarke and Ray Stanfield for generously sharing their collections.

The business was founded in1880 by Thomas Horsfall Midwood and was continued by his son, Charles until his death in 1948. Other family members played a role too - Mary Midwood (Charles's daughter) recalls working in the shop and studio on South Promenade, next to the RNLI Station, during the busy summer season, selling Midwood postcards, taking print orders, and using a fine paint brush and coloured inks to tint the prints.

The subject matter was extraordinary in its breadth, recording both joyful and solemn occasions, from yachts sailing serenely in Ramsey Bay, to ships dashed on the rocks in stormy seas.

There are royal visits, grand civic occasions, carnivals and regattas, the first motorcycle races, the arrival of the Manx Electric Railway, floods and heavy snow, sporting successes, weddings, tea parties, cattle marts and fish markets, portraits and tranquil rural scenes.

A big part of Ramsey's history is here. As it has often been noted, without the Midwood family, we would not have this unique insight into the town as it was, with people and buildings that are no longer with us.

Tom Midwood was born in Ramsey. His father was originally from Cheshire, settled in Ramsey and married a Miss Horsfall. They lived in Mona Street.

After leaving school, Tom worked in the cotton business in Manchester, but returned to Ramsey when aged about 20 and started business as a photographer.

When he passed away, aged 68, on Good Friday (April 15, 1927), the *Ramsey Courier* described him as *'one of the most valued and beloved citizens of the town'.*

The obituary continued:

Tom Midwood was one of 'nature's gentlemen'. Always courteous and pleasant of speech, he was the same in his attitude to rich and poor alike, and all found in him that gentleness of disposition and sympathy of heart which made him easily one of the most popular men in our little community.

'At his studio on the Promenade in the summer, year by year, he had literally scores of friends who always came to greet him, and his genial smile and good humour were infectious. He contributed in many ways to the pleasure of the visitors who regarded him as a friend'.

He truly was 'a man of the people' - a magistrate, town commissioner, Poor Law Guardian, chairman of the Lifeboat Committee, secretary of the Cottage Hospital, sidesman at St Paul's Church, Freemason, and Oddfellow.

It was said that, in all his undertakings, he displayed calm judgment, tact and patience - qualities that also enhanced his skills as a photographer.

He and his wife Alice had seven children: Tommy, who died in Gallipoli during WW1, George who worked in Lloyd's Bank, Ramsey, also died young; Charles, the eldest, and Taylor, a chemist, both served in the Great War. In addition, there were three daughters.

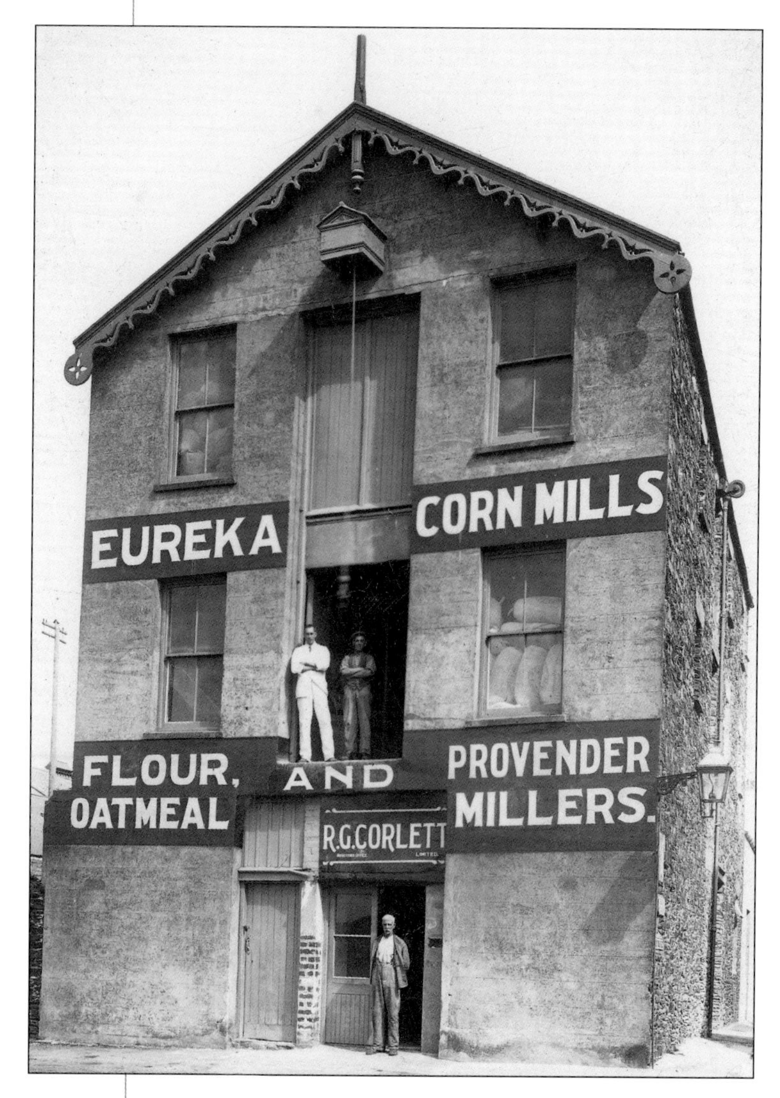

Eureka Corn Mills on East Quay is currently occupied by Mezeron. It was opened in 1932 by brothers Gilbert and Norman Corlett, who installed a small Tattersall mill. Gilbert went on to form R.G. Corlett Ltd., which acquired Laxey Flour Mills.

C.J. Midwood

Charles James Midwood continued the business after his father's death. He was a keen sportsman, equally gifted at football and golf. With his father, he conducted Midwood's billiard saloon in Mona Street, which was a popular centre at one time. He served on the Lifeboat Committee and belonged to Ramsey branch of the British Legion and also served with the Manx Volunteers.

Mr Midwood had extensive connections throughout the North, especially in sporting circles and was noted for his excellent shots of the TT Races.

After his death in 1948 aged 67 the business closed.

Thomas Horsfall Midwood.

Acknowledgments
This book would not have been possible without Les Clarke and Ray Stanfield, for so generously sharing their unique postcard collections with us. Thanks also to Richard Radcliffe, Nigel Malpass and Raymond Jopson for their contributions.

Sources consulted:

The Story of Laxey Flour, Andrew Scarffe (Manx Experience, 2010)
Portrait of the Isle of Man, Canon Stenning (Robt. Hale Ltd., 1958)
Manx Inns, Suzanne Cubbon (Amulree Publications, 1998)
Our Heritage, Kate Rodgers (1995)
A Postcard Tour, S. Dearden & K. Hassall (Stenlake Publications, 1995)
Andreas, Sally McCambridge (2005)
Shining by the Sea, Constance Radcliffe (Nelson Press, 1989)
Manx Millennium Supplement (IOM Examiner, 2000)
A Sulby Heritage Trail by Juan Vernon (2009)
The Ramsey Lifeboats by W.N. Seybold, (Nelson Press,1991)

Ascog Hall, a large flat-iron type building at the apex of Stanley Mount East and West. Built in the early 1900s as The Albion residential hotel, it was requisitioned in WWII to accommodate guards from the Mooragh Internment Camp.

The Ramsey Café, Parliament Street – next door was Lay's the tailors and Cleators', drapers.

Ramsey's first Catholic church, pictured, was demolished in 1909 to make way for the new one; the far wall was retained and can be seen where the shrine of Our Lady, Star of the Sea, now stands.

North Shore Road with Wesleyan Chapel on right. The chapel was built in 1891 on land given by Susannah Gibson, daughter of the shipyard owner. It functioned as a place of worship until 1913 when it became a recreation room for the National Children's Home at Ballacloan. The spire has been removed, but the inscribed foundation stone can still be seen amongst the weeds.

Sheep grazing in the field in front of Westbourne Road houses – before the Bus Station was built.

Ramsey's famous Swing Bridge was built in 1892 at a cost £50,000– a sum far in excess of that originally anticipated. In the foreground we see 'the patent slip', constructed at the Shipyard in 1856 to enable vessels of all sizes to discharge cargo at all times of the tide.

East Quay, Ramsey in the snow. Clague's Foundry office, with arched door, was purchased in 1913 by the I.O.M. Steam Packet Company.

Army reservists arrived in their thousands in the years before and after World War One and set up training camps at the Mooragh, Claughbane and Glen Auldyn. They were welcomed not least for the significant contribution they made to the local economy. Here we see the 53rd Welsh Camp, 1925, from Skye Hill.

Cronk Ruagh Isolation Hospital, Jurby Road opened in 1896. It was a sanatorium from 1930 – 1962 and served as the elderly people's wing of Ramsey Cottage Hospital from 1964 – 1982. It is now the site of luxury homes.

St Mary's Church, Ballaugh, with overgrown gateway.

Changing face of Parliament Street. These vehicles are driven by engines, not pulled by horses.

Horse-drawn coaches waiting for arrivals at Queen's Pier. The original Victorian wooden tollhouses were replaced by the present drab buildings in the 1950s.

North Ramsey, corner of Sandy (now Bowring) Road and Windsor Road.

Windmills are rare in the Isle of Man, but one example is Monk's Mill, Jurby Road, Ramsey, built in the 1840s for grinding corn. With its top levelled, it became a private residence called Beaconsfield Towers. In more recent times it has been incorporated into a residential home for the elderly.

The Home of Rest on the right, was originally a private residence called Rhodesia House. It opened as a nursing home in the 1930s. It is now called Grove Mount Residential Home.

The Plaza, seen at the far end of Peel Street, was built in 1891 as the Ramsey Palace and functioned as a theatre, concert hall and cinema, run on temperance principles. It was remodelled and re-named the Plaza in 1935. It closed in 1974 and was demolished in 1990. The site is now a car park.

Clague's foundry, East Quay manufactured all sorts of cast iron items, including most of the fittings and fixtures on the Queen's Pier.

St Paul's Church, facing on to Market Square, dates back to 1822. The present porch was added in 1938.

Market Hill about 1910. The building on the right hand corner is Corlett's Bakery, later Tyson's sweet shop, beyond which is Jones's sewing machine shop and Callow & Sons, jewellers.

Queen's Hotel, Stanley Mount was conveniently situated opposite the Pier. It was destroyed by fire in April 1983 and the site has since been redeveloped as an apartment block.

The Hydro in 1890s, when Ramsey was sometimes called the 'Naples of Manxland'. The hotel was later re-named the Grand Island and had a chequered history until it was finally demolished in 2009.

Chauffeured cars await the gentry in Parliament Street. Wattleworth's Café on the right was a popular place to meet for morning coffee or afternoon tea.

Mona-ville (later Beach Hotel) boasted 'fine views of sea and land'. It is now part of the Fountains apartment complex.

Carriages await passenger arrivals at Queen's Pier.

Tar boiler and steam roller carrying out improvements to Market Square. A new programme to regenerate what is now called 'Market Place' is currently under consideration!

Ballure Shore in the 1890s was designated the 'Ladies' Bathing Shore'. Note the bathing huts in the background.

Holidaymakers taking a stroll along South Promenade. Houses and shops on the left were demolished in the 1960s.

The Open-air Swimming Baths on Mooragh Promenade was a popular venue in the summer season. Galas and diving demonstrations were among the attractions.

Suffragettes addressing holidaymakers on south shore, Ramsey. In 1881, the Isle of Man was the first country in the world to grant women the right to vote in national elections. This would have pleased Emmeline Pankhurst, leader of the British Suffragette movement, whose mother was of Manx ancestry (courtesy of Ken Hassell).

Queen's Promenade: on the left can be seen the Prince of Wales Hotel, the Norbury Boathouse and, under the arcade, Midwood's shop.

Pierrot shows on the south shore were a twice-daily attraction in Edwardian times. Note Clague's Foundry chimney on the left.

Queen's Promenade with the Prince of Wales Hotel (right), built in 1849 as a private residence named Marine Mansion. It is now private apartments.

It's those Pierrots again…

Straw boaters for the men and parasols for the ladies when taking a stroll along South Prom.

Pierrots provided family entertainment twice daily on the south beach.

Making sandcastles on the South shore.

Children enjoying a donkey ride on South Prom, just in front of Midwood's shop.

Mooragh Promenade and North beach. The grassy area is now designated an ASSI - area of special scientific interest.

Youngsters having a 'splashing time' in the children's pool.

Sulby Glen Hotel: horse-drawn carriages based at the hotel carried summer visitors as far as Tholt-y-Will, and further afield to Snaefell.

Kirk Andreas Rectory dates, in part, to the mid-1600s. It served as a youth hostel in the days when thousands of holiday-makers explored the Island on foot or bicycle.

Old Ballaugh. Card posted 21st September 1909 to W.H. Lunn Esq., Chateau Saguenay, Chicoutin, Quebec, Canada.

Spring Bank Cottage, beside Ballamanaugh bridge, Sulby.

Main Road, Ballaugh in the days when ponies and traps were more common than motor vehicles.

Glen Villas, Sulby is a fine, private residence with beautiful grounds, where church garden fetes have been held over the years.

Maughold village, with its 14th century parish cross standing where it stood until 1937 when it was moved into the churchyard. It now stands inside the church, protected from the elements.

Watering the cattle at Kella Mill dam, Sulby.

Bride village post mistress from 1897-1920 was Esther Christian. She was succeeded by her daughter, Esther (Kinrade), who ran it until 1963.

Monday was Mart Day in Ramsey, when farmers from all over the northern plain came to buy and sell livestock.

Long, low thatched cottage near the shore at Port Mooar is now a holiday home.

Ballamoar Castle, Jurby, former home of a controversial figure, Dr Alexander Cannon, was the location for this large gathering, celebrating the Coronation of George V.

Main Road, Ballaugh with Albert Hotel in the distance.
(Ray Stansfield Collection)

Hawthorn Cottage, Maughold village. The hedge is much higher today.

Andreas Parish Church, built in the 1860s. The original tower stood 120ft high, but its height was halved in 1940s when it was deemed to be a hazard to wartime aircraft.

Maughold Lighthouse, under construction, 1914.

Sulby village at the turn of the last century, around the time when the artist, Archibald Knox occupied a cottage on the left. It was a highly productive phase in his career and he posted hundreds of designs to Liberty's & Co., of London from the post and telegraph office opposite.

Port Lewaigue was first developed as a residential area in 1885 when Mr Humphrey Lloyd of Manchester bought 10 acres and laid it out for building, following it with a much larger portion in 1900.

Port Mooar: the wooden café in the foreground, which had swings and see-saws for the children, was run by George Logan, who also sold refreshments from a stall at Albert Tower.

Maughold lighthouse. Construction started in April 1911 and the lighthouse began its work on 15th April 1914. The first Principal Keeper was a Mr Quine, a Manx speaker from the south. Today, the lighthouse is automated.

Andreas School pupils 1922.

Pastoral idyll - Sulby Glen.

'Greenlands' on the banks of the Sulby river was a popular picnic and boating area on the outskirts of Ramsey.

Dhoon Glen Hotel, erected 1882, caught alight one Sunday afternoon in 1932. Ramsey Fire Brigade was soon on the scene, but the building's timber construction and the difficulty of getting a water supply hampered efforts to save it. The site today is used for parking.

Rural scene, Sulby.

Tholt-y-Will tearooms, Sulby Glen.

Miss Evelyn Boston of Andreas driving the first petrol tractor on the Island. The picture was taken at the IOM Agricultural Society Show, held in a field on Lezayre Road in August 1916. The tractor was owned by show president, Mr J.J. Christian, of Braust.

Thatched cottages by the village green, Old Sulby.

St Jude's, with ivy-clad tower, was consecrated in November 1841 as a chapel-of-ease to the parish church at Kirk Andreas.

Horse and cart being led through the pretty village of Bride.

S.S. Little Orme, en route from Irvine to Douglas with a cargo of bricks, went aground at Cranstal, Bride in November 1936. The crew of five were rescued by Ramsey Rocket Brigade. The vessel was re-floated with help from *S.S. Ben Ellan*.

S.S. Donegal, a Midland Railway Co. ship on passage from Heysham to Belfast ran aground near the gravel pit jetty at the Point of Ayre in thick fog on 8th October 1908. Her sister ship, S.S. Antrim (aided by the S.S. Ellan Vannin) helped her to refloat.

'Fishing fleet, Ramsey' is the title of this postcard.

Topsail schooner, *Maggie Barratt*, makes its way into Ramsey harbour.

Sailing boats moored at East Quay drying their sails in the sun.

Sails reflected in calm waters.

This iconic image shows how Ramsey harbour has changed over the years.

Loading turnips for export at the quayside. Turnips (sometimes called 'moots') were introduced into the Island at the end of the 1700s and were found to be well-suited to the climate. In 1899 it was recorded that the Island's main exports were 'barley, turnips and potatoes'.

A serious accident occurred at a launching exercise of Ramsey lifeboat on 1st September 1913. One of the axles of the launching carriage broke and a wheel fell off, injuring a male spectator who was carried by stretcher to the waiting ambulance. He later received £100 in compensation.

Old view of Ramsey harbour. RY1 *Hearts of Oak*.

Passengers alight from a steamer at the Queen's Pier. The last steamer called at the pier head in 1970.

A cartload of hay – to provide fodder for horses in the busy port of Liverpool – being loaded onto a sailing boat at West Quay. Note the train tracks, laid down in 1892, principally to haul wagons loaded with coal from the quayside to the train station.

'Nickeys' and 'nobbies' were the most common type of fishing boat to sail out of Ramsey a century ago. They were superseded by steam trawlers, which few could afford and were more difficult to manage.

Ben-my-Chree berthing at the Queen's Pier. Steam Packet vessels carrying holidaymakers called at Ramsey for many years. The last time was in 1970.

Naming ceremony of Ramsey lifeboat, *Lady Harrison*, 16th July 1931. This vessel was in service until 1948 and during that period was engaged in 48 rescues resulting in 93 lives being saved.

Christmas poultry display at one of several butchers' shops in Ramsey in the days before supermarkets. A trade directory for 1894 lists John Brew, Bourne Place; Edward Cubbon, Church Street; John Wade and daughter Frances, Bourne Place.

The message on the reverse of this card reads: 'Evelyn Vondy, mother of Joyce and Yvonne, as May Queen outside her father's grocery shop.'

A carnival parade sets off from the Mitre Hotel, Parliament Street. Colourful processions such as this were a regular feature of the holiday season.

Back row: Thomas Midwood, Mildred Mary Midwood, George Midwood, Marion Alice Midwood.
Front row: Edith Midwood, T H Midwood, Alice Midwood, Charles James Midwood.
Ground: Harry Taylor Midwood.

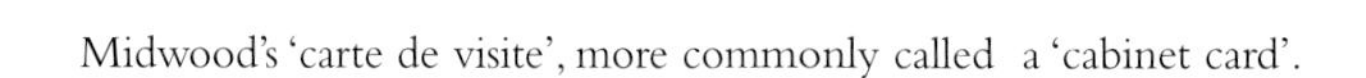

Midwood's 'carte de visite', more commonly called a 'cabinet card'.

Betsy Kinnin, in white apron, ready to auction a large catch landed at the 'fish steps', East Quay. The Kinnins are one of Ramsey's oldest families. The Salt Works' chimneys in the background date this to after 1912, which is the year they were constructed.

Sulby Claddagh was as popular with picnickers in Edwardian times as it is today.

Market Square was the location of this large gathering, but what was the occasion? The drinking fountain in the centre commemorates the establishment of the town commissioners in 1865.

Alexandra Rose Day gathering outside Midwood's shop, 26th June 1912, marking the 50th anniversary of the Danish princess's arrival in Britain for her marriage to King Edward VII. Artificial roses made by people with disabilities were sold to help the sick and the needy. The charity is still active today.

A May Queen parade. T.H. Midwood was chairman of the town commissioners and vice-president of the May Day Committee from 1908-10.

Coronation Day parade 1953. R.G. Corlett's 'Peter Pan' entry won a first prize.

Rule Britannia! Empire Day procession assembles in Queen's Drive. Note the billboard advertising the Imperial Hotel on South Promenade.

Horse-drawn carriage carrying the carnival queen waits outside the Mitre for the start of the grand parade.

Arts & crafts display. This is thought to have been taken in the Queen's Hall at a fundraiser for the new Catholic Church.

An 'old salt' taking a rest on the quayside.

Ramsey had its own 'bellman' (town crier), to make public announcements. This is Philip Corlett, bellman from 1902–27.

Thomas Horsfall Midwood (right) and local coach proprietor Ned Dawson (left) 'having a yarn' on a seat in front of the Midwood shop.

Corlett's bread van outside 33 Parliament Street in 1914.

Edwardian gentleman inspecting the catch on East Quay.

Johnson's Store's bread delivery lad.

Carnival parade congregates in Queen's Drive.

A big catch being inspected at the Fishing Steps on the corner of East Quay.

Sir Hall Caine, famous novelist and MHK for Ramsey attending Tynwald with the Lieutenant Governor, Lord Raglan.

'Empire Day' carnival float outside the Union Hotel (now the Harbour Bistro) on the north-east corner of Market Place and East Quay. Empire Day was celebrated on 24th May each year until the 1950s when the empire began to decline.

Grand Opening of Ramsey Cottage Hospital in 1904.

J.S. Kneale's – one of many butcher shops in 'old Ramsey'.

Negotiating the Hairpin in a horse and trap was a tricky business, whether going up or down!

People gathered on the quayside when fresh fish were laid out ready for auction. Mrs Kinnin is clearly recognisable in her trade mark white apron.

Ramsey Cottage Hospital nurses line up in Parliament Square for presentation to visiting royalty.

W.D. Clark, family butcher, at the junction of Bowring Road and North Shore Road.

Another view of the fish market.

King George V and Queen Mary at Bishopscourt during the royal visit of 1920.

Tailoring staff at the rear of Lay's, gents' outfitters, Parliament Street.

James Gelling's butcher shop, Church Street.

Manx Electric Railway permanent way gang take a rest from track maintenance, Maughold.

Birds' eye view from Lherghy Frissell of a tram crossing Ballure Bridge.

The Manx Electric Railway opening at Ballure, 2nd August 1898. *(Ray Stansfield Collection)*

The MER line from Laxey to Ballure was officially opened by the Lieutenant Governor, Lord Henniker on 2nd August, 1898. At the end of the season, work immediately started on building a bridge across the glen to allow the tram to travel into the town. The bridge was officially opened in July 1899 and a regular half-hourly service, from 7am – 9pm, was established. *(Ray Stansfield Collection)*

A cyclist travels over the railway tracks in Station Road, Kirk Michael. The Manx Northern Railway Company began in 1879, with trains running from St John's through Kirk Michael, Ballaugh and Sulby. *(Ray Stansfield Collection)*

Tram passing below the towering guest houses of Brookhill.

Manx Northern Railway trains were carried over the river at Ballakilingan by an 88-ft long wrought- iron girder bridge, referred to as the 'Basket Bridge' because of the arch-shaped stretcher connecting its bowstrings. When the IOM Railway Company took over in 1906 strengthening work was carried out. The bridge continued to give cause for concern and was replaced by a lattice steel girder structure in 1914.

Although the name is obscured from view, this looks like engine No. 3 Pender, ready to depart from the platform on the south side of Ramsey station.

A Wickham railcar was operated by the IOM Harbour Board along the length of the Queen's Pier for many years. A record number of 36,000 passengers used the pier in 1906.
(Ray Stansfield Collection)

Ballure Mount lashed by storm waves. Midwood needed an abundance of patience and skill to capture this dramatic moment.

The Latvian barque, 'Austrums', carrying a cargo of pitch, went aground in a severe gale off the Point of Ayre on 26th January 1927while en route from Runcorn to San Sebastian, Spain. All nine crew were taken to safety by the Rocket Brigade, but the ship was a total loss.

The steamship HMS Doon went aground in stormy seas, north of Ramsey, 18th November 1930.

Quayside flooding caused by strong winds and high tides is nothing new. The high-stepping horse in the background seems to be trying to keep his hooves dry.

Church Street, knee-deep in water in February 1925 when a combination of gales and spring tides caused flooding. The area was demolished in the South Ramsey re-development scheme of the 1960s/70s.

Fleetwood trawler *SS Cevic* ran aground near Port Lewaigue in 1927. The vessel was a total loss but all the crew members survived. The wreckage can still be seen at low tide.

The steam trawler *Merisia* sank in Bulgham Bay in January 1940. The boat was part of the Fleetwood fishing fleet on passage to the Isle of Man when she became overwhelmed by huge waves and was grounded on rocks in Bulgham Bay with the loss of all 12 crew. The ship's bell was recovered in recent years and is displayed at Ramsey lifeboat station. *(Ray Stansfield Collection)*

Bourne Place in the snow. Saddle Buildings (right) incorporating the Saddle Hotel and adjacent shops were built in the 1890s by Boddington's brewery.

'After the storm, Glen Auldyn'. A calm and peaceful September evening in 1930 was disrupted by a sudden storm with flash floods. Gale force winds blew down trees and the Auldyn river broke its banks, causing widespread damage to property and the road surface.

Surveying the damage after the floods in Glen Auldyn, September 1930.

Parliament Street in the Great Snow of February 1895 when it snowed incessantly for 33 hours!

Bourne Place in the snow. The popular Cingalee café is on the left.

Clearing the snow in Dale Street, South Ramsey.

Parliament Street in the snow.

Sidecar passes the Castrol garage, Ballaugh on a circuit of the TT course.
(Ray Stansfield Collection)

Midwood was usually present at important sporting events in the north. Here he captures Vick rounding the Hairpin in the TT.

The Gordon Bennett hill climb for motor vehicles was held for the first time in 1904. The half-mile course ran from Port Lewaigue to Maughold village.

A 1910 15hp Rover stops for a photo outside Midwood's.

Rowing race held on the river by the Stone Bridge, Ramsey. The bridge was built in 1755, widened in 1840, and underwent further improvements in 1888.

Gordon-Bennett Motor Car Road Racing trials, first run in the Isle of Man in 1904, were the precursor of the world famous TT races.

Ramsey Golf Club was formed in September 1891. Some months later, a General Brereton inaugurated the nine-hole links, which constitutes the Milntown side of the course.

A. Tinkler at Ramsey Hairpin.

Sidecar rounding the Hairpin.

Gordon Bennett time trials – car No. 9 – a Napier.

Humber stand at an early car racing event, outside Albert Road School.